D0031886

THE IMPACT OF SLAVERY
IN AMERICA

By Duchess Harris, JD, PhD
with Gail Radley

Essential Library

An Imprint of Abdo Publishing | abdobooks.com

Published by Abdo Publishing, a division of ABDO, PO Box 398166, Minneapolis, Minnesota 55439. Copyright © 2020 by Abdo Consulting Group, Inc. International copyrights reserved in all countries. No part of this book may be reproduced in any form without written permission from the publisher. Essential Library™ is a trademark and logo of Abdo Publishing.

Printed in the United States of America, North Mankato, Minnesota.
042019
092019

THIS BOOK CONTAINS RECYCLED MATERIALS

Cover Photo: National Archives/Newsmakers/Hulton Archive/Getty Images
Interior Photos: Stock Montage/Archive Photos/Getty Images, 4–5; iStockphoto, 6, 66–67, 96; Everett Historical/Shutterstock Images, 11, 12, 14–15, 18, 54–55, 59; Atlanta Journal-Constitution/AP Images, 21; Circa Images/Glasshouse Images/SuperStock, 22; Pantheon/SuperStock, 24; Robert Abbott Sengstacke/The Abbott Sengstacke Family Papers/Archive Photos/Getty Images, 27; API/Gamma-Rapho/Getty Images, 32–33; AP Images, 35, 73, 83; Rich Fury/Invision/AP Images, 39; Everett Collection/Newscom, 42–43; James D'Alba/AP Images, 47; Red Line Editorial, 53; Richard B. Levine/Newscom, 63; David Goldman/AP Images, 71; Rebecca Cook/Reuters/Newscom, 77; Shutterstock Images, 78–79; Jacqueline Larma/AP Images, 84; Douliery Olivier/Abacapress.com/Sipa/AP Images, 88–89; John Gomez/Alamy, 94

Editor: Alyssa Krekelberg
Series Designer: Laura Graphenteen

LIBRARY OF CONGRESS CONTROL NUMBER: 2018966045

PUBLISHER'S CATALOGING-IN-PUBLICATION DATA

Names: Harris, Duchess, author | Radley, Gail, author.
Title: The impact of slavery in America / by Duchess Harris and Gail Radley
Description: Minneapolis, Minnesota : Abdo Publishing, 2020 | Series: Slavery in America | Includes online resources and index.
Identifiers: ISBN 9781532119255 (lib. bdg.) | ISBN 9781532173431 (ebook)
Subjects: LCSH: Slavery--United States--History--Juvenile literature. | African Americans--United States--Juvenile literature. | Whites--United States--Relations with African Americans--Juvenile literature. | Racism--United States--Juvenile literature.
Classification: DDC 326.9--dc23

CONTENTS

CHAPTER ONE

FIGHTING TO BE FREE

Charles Deslondes, an enslaved man, had a dangerous secret: he was planning a rebellion. Deslondes had special privileges and responsibilities on a plantation. For years, he was a plantation driver, watching over enslaved people toiling in the fields and whipping them. He also helped hunt down escapees. The slaveholder trusted him, but Deslondes longed for freedom and to free those he had been forced to abuse.

Louisiana, where Deslondes lived, was well known for its inhumane treatment of enslaved people. "Slaves worked longer hours, faced more brutal punishments, and lived shorter lives than any other slave society in North America," notes Daniel

Enslaved people had to plan their uprisings in secret.

Toussaint Louverture won many victories during the Haitian Revolution.

Rasmussen, author of *American Uprising*.[1] People enslaved in the more northern border states dreaded being sold to the deep South.

But a thin thread of hope ran through slave quarters in Louisiana and beyond. In the French-Caribbean colony of Saint-Domingue, known today as Haiti, formerly enslaved Toussaint Louverture had led an army of black people to independence from European colonizers in the late 1790s and early 1800s. Throughout the slave states, many captives dreamed of, sang about, and planned for rebellion, escape, and freedom. Deslondes waited, plotted, and chose partners carefully. Escaping was not enough, he felt. Appeals to justice or mercy wouldn't win enslaved people their freedom. Plantation owners relied on them too much for running the plantations, providing meals and clothing for their families, and sending the South's products to market. The slaves who ran would be hunted, tortured, and killed to discourage others from rebelling. For their own territory, and for freedom, Deslondes reasoned, they would have to fight.

THE ATTACK

Deslondes and his men chose January 8, 1811, for their attack. They picked this date because planters would be celebrating an annual carnival and the US military was busy fighting the Spaniards. Spain controlled part of Louisiana at the time, and the United States wanted it. Deslondes's slaveholder, Manuel Andry, and his adult son, both militiamen, were sleeping

WHEN COTTON WAS KING

Plantations produced many goods, including hemp, rice, sugar, and tobacco. But during slavery, cotton was the king of crops. Although New England, Britain, and many countries in Europe abolished the slave trade in the early 1800s, they still bought slave-produced cotton. Cotton brought white people a lot of money, and the South was intent on preserving the system of slavery that produced it. As historian Gene Dattel explains it, "Cotton prolonged America's most serious social tragedy, slavery, and slave-produced cotton caused the American Civil War."[2]

when the rebels burst in, armed with axes, sugarcane knives, and other makeshift weapons. They killed Andry's son, while Andry, blood streaming from long cuts, fled into the night.

The rebels outfitted themselves with uniforms, muskets, and ammunition. They planned to take New Orleans, Louisiana, burning plantations along the way. Word spread as they headed toward the city. They were joined by other people from nearby plantations.

Some enslaved people believed this rebellion would fail as others had. They had seen the heads of rebels mounted on pikes to rot. Believing their loyalty might be rewarded with freedom, some told the slaveholders of the scheme. Word spread among white people. Many whites hid in nearby swamps or waited out the trouble elsewhere.

The warning also reached New Orleans, and a militia organized. On January 10, the two sides faced off in a sugarcane field. Too soon, though, the rebels' ammunition was spent, and casualties mounted. Numerous rebels were slaughtered there. Others fled, and many were captured. Deslondes ran into the swamps where bloodhounds caught him. He was returned to the field and killed. Most captives met the same fate, and their heads were displayed as a warning to other would-be rebels.

Rasmussen describes Deslondes's rebellion as "the largest slave revolt in American history," yet the event is not well known.[3] Reports downplayed the size and determination of Deslondes's army. In truth, the uprising stunned Louisiana planters, who feared it might inspire others.

DREAMS OF FREEDOM

The lack of official coverage did not stop the stories. Other, better-known rebellions followed. In 1831, Nat Turner led more than 40 enslaved people in Virginia from plantation to plantation, killing some 55 whites. The rebellion was quashed, and 55 people were executed, including Turner, who was hanged and skinned. Like Deslondes's uprising, Turner's stirred fear and anger among whites. Nearly 200 other blacks, many uninvolved with Turner's rebellion, were slaughtered by mobs.[4] Yet the violent and often horrifying responses did not discourage

KOOK AND QUAMANA

African-born Kook and Quamana, two of Deslondes's partners, were likely captured warriors sold to slavers. They survived the horrific ocean journey to find themselves on a Louisiana plantation in 1806. Quickly, the men began searching for other enslaved people who would join their fight for freedom. Kook and Quamana argued passionately to win support. Once the rebellion was squelched, Kook and Quamana were among the rebels who were tried, executed, and decapitated.

Nat Turner and Freedom

Long before Nat Turner staged his rebellion, many of his fellow slaves felt he was intended for something great. Intelligent and religious, he often spent free moments praying and fasting. As a young man in the 1820s, Turner had various visions. One vision showed blood on corn and figures formed in blood. After that, Turner said he was instructed to prepare to fight slavery. Turner believed that he must "slay [his] enemies with their own weapons."[5]

future uprisings. Historians have found evidence of hundreds of slave rebellions.

African Americans were not entirely alone in fighting for their freedom. While many white abolitionists helped fleeing slaves travel north while demanding slavery's end, another white man, John Brown, tried war. In 1859, Brown led more than a dozen men, both black and white, to capture West Virginia's Harpers Ferry Armory and other government buildings. The armory was a national site for manufacturing weapons. Brown and his men hoped to distribute weapons to the city's enslaved population, but the US Marines overwhelmed them. Despite Brown's failure, war would soon come—the Civil War (1861–1865), which pitted North against South.

Dreams of freedom grew through such stories of bravery. At that time, most people seeking slavery's end believed, like Brown, that only war would work.

John Brown's forces wanted to provoke a slave rebellion. Brown was arrested and hanged for his actions.

During the war, enslaved people fled by the hundreds to Virginia's Fort Monroe and to other Union strongholds within Confederate territory. Some slaveholders wanted enslaved people to fight for the South. Rather than allow that to happen, Union officers gave enslaved people refuge. "By the war's end," reports Christopher Beagan for the National Park Service, "approximately half a million freedom-seekers had fled to Union lines."[6] However, some of the officers still regarded them as slaves. Enslaved people were popularly called contrabands—meaning they were neither slave nor free. The men among them were given the chance to fight for the North, but they were not

Abraham Lincoln was determined to keep the Union together.

entirely welcome. Northern soldiers often thought they would be unreliable in battle, but black soldiers proved their bravery.

FREE BY LAW

On January 1, 1863, President Abraham Lincoln signed into law the Emancipation Proclamation, declaring freedom from slavery for some people. The new law carved out certain limits. It affected only those states that had joined the Confederacy, and some slave states had not joined. Confederate slave states already fallen to the North could keep their slaves. The remaining Confederate states battled on, hoping to defeat Lincoln's order, because if the North lost the war, the order would mean nothing.

As African Americans fought, they gained a sense of their own power and demanded more rights. Some took over plantations and imprisoned former slaveholders in their homes, while others demanded release of their still-enslaved wives. Lincoln eventually granted the soldiers their freedom.

To most Southern whites, the world had gone mad and the natural order of things had been reversed. They depended on slave labor to manage their crops and run their households. Whites had convinced themselves that blacks' role was to serve them. The legacy of white Southern beliefs and actions has stretched into the present day, deeply affecting nearly every aspect of African Americans' lives and shaping white lives as well.

DISCUSSION STARTERS

- Do you think slavery would have ended without the Civil War? Why or why not? How much longer might it have taken?

- Why do you think Southern plantation owners valued their wealth and cotton-based economy over human rights?

- What does the Northern soldiers' reluctance to fight alongside black soldiers suggest about their beliefs and experiences?

CHAPTER TWO

THE LONG ROAD TOWARD EQUALITY

Southerners felt that if enslaved people could no longer be forced to work in whites' fields and households after the Civil War—which the North won—then a similar system had to be devised. The Black Codes, enacted immediately after the war's end, closely matched slavery. Although states' details varied, the codes' effect was to require formerly enslaved people to be employed by a white person—usually the former slaveholder—and eliminate other means of earning a living. South Carolina forbade African Americans from leaving their plantations or having visitors, and Florida's law even demanded they obey and

Many African American families struggled to start new lives after the Civil War.

show respect to employers. The North quickly objected to this practice, passing the Fourteenth Amendment to the US Constitution in 1868. This amendment gave former slaves US citizenship and restricted states from denying citizens their rights.

FORMATION OF THE KKK

White Southerners were unhappy about this radically new society. They had once been the sole rulers of their society, but now Northerners had reorganized their lives, and their former slaves were voting and becoming politicians. Historian Eric Foner estimates that following the war, during Reconstruction (1865–1877), approximately 2,000 African American men held public offices.[1] Many of them were former slaves.

Just after the war's end, six discontented Confederate soldiers discussed their problems at a Tennessee bar. They formed a social club intended for "Chivalry, Humanity, Mercy and Patriotism." They planned to "protect the weak, innocent, and defenseless."[2] They called their group the Ku Klux Klan (KKK). The Klan quickly drew many members and admirers. It also grew violent and began spreading terror. In 1868, the KKK killed three African American legislators in South Carolina and another in Arkansas.[3] When African Americans held an election parade in Camilla, Georgia, the sheriff himself led hundreds of

STRUGGLING TO VOTE

Women were barred from voting until 1920, but after the Civil War, black men swelled the Southern voting polls. White Southerners were alarmed to find former slaves elected to Congress and occupying local positions. They sought to reestablish white supremacy. They committed violence and used other tactics to discourage African American voters. Often, Southern states demanded they pass more difficult literacy tests than were required of white voters and pay poll taxes. Another method, called gerrymandering, draws political boundaries to benefit one side. For example, drawing lines through an African American community can lessen their votes' impact. A major part of the civil rights struggle involved securing African American voting rights. Even today, people of color are more often removed from voting lists than whites and face more obstacles, such as strict voter ID laws, longer lines, and lack of nearby polling places.

Klansmen in a fury of gunfire. Klansmen accomplished their goal: voters were discouraged from exercising their rights, and the pro-Confederate Democrats regained power in five Southern states. Encouraged, 500 Klansmen also lynched eight African Americans held in a South Carolina jail.[4]

The reign of terror sputtered out as President Ulysses S. Grant rallied Congress to enforce African Americans' rights. In 1871, the Ku Klux Klan Act passed, allowing use of the military against terrorist groups that interfered with Fourteenth Amendment rights. Months later, troops were sent into some troublesome South

The KKK is known as a hate group.

Carolina counties. Black and white citizens in the Carolinas also fought the Klan. The federal government treated Klan actions as rebellion against the nation, arresting hundreds, trying leaders, and sending many to prison. The KKK grew quiet by 1872, but it would reorganize in 1915. In the 1920s, women began participating in the Klan. The women's KKK had more than one million members.[5]

Part of its mission was to organize youth groups to push the KKK's beliefs.

Racial violence continued. The Equal Justice Initiative (EJI) found that more than 4,000 lynchings occurred between 1877 and 1950 in 12 Southern states.[6] Most victims were African American, but some were white supporters. And not all lynchings took place in the South. The EJI also found more than 300 lynchings elsewhere.[7] As EJI comments on its website, lynchings often didn't even require a crime. Many people were lynched "for bumping into a white person, or wearing their military uniforms after World War I [1914–1918], or not using the appropriate title when addressing a white person."[8] Lynchings were usually public, and these crimes typically went unpunished.

WHITE SUPREMACY

People who supported slavery and then the second-class citizenship of black people argued that Africans and their descendants were not human. Therefore, they could be kept and sold like livestock. They viewed slaves as property rather than as people. Thus, whites felt they could largely ignore black people's thoughts and feelings, and even their physical needs. Whites also thought blacks might be taught through severe punishment.

Two schools of thought assisted white supremacy. Slaveholders used the first, religion, to support their interests, emphasizing obedience and whites' superior status. Whites continued to preach the supposed God-given status of white rule long after slavery's end.

Second, the science of the mid-1800s and onward also supported white supremacy's agenda. These scientists set out to prove that Africans were inferior, drawing on observations of small groups. Now termed *scientific racism*, this science ignored social, political, and other influences in shaping people. It appealed to many whites, both in the North and South, who were disturbed by African Americans taking fuller roles in society.

ENTER JIM CROW

Bolstered by the era's pseudoscience, the discarded Black Codes were reformed in a tangle of restrictions known as Jim Crow laws, which started in 1877. Jim Crow was a black caricature, dreamed up and performed by a white man who blackened his face to entertain whites in minstrel shows. His foolishness supported white beliefs about African American inferiority.

Jim Crow laws touched nearly every public experience African Americans had. Homer Plessy knew this too well when he stepped into a whites-only railroad car in 1892. Having a white parent, he was light-skinned enough that

The civil rights movement in the 1950s and 1960s fought against Jim Crow laws.

the conductor asked if he was "a colored man." When Plessy answered that he was, he was told to leave. "I am an American citizen," replied Plessy. "I have paid for a

People of color were forced to use many separate areas during the Jim Crow era. For example, they had to use different water coolers than whites.

first-class ticket, and intend to ride . . . in the first-class car."[9] He was dragged from the train and arrested.

Plessy wanted to test Louisiana's separate seating law in the courts. The 1875 Civil Rights Act outlawed discrimination. But in 1896, in *Plessy v. Ferguson*, the Supreme Court ignored the clearly inferior services provided for African Americans and argued that discrimination didn't exist if separate but equal services were provided.

In addition to discriminatory laws, a web of social customs continually reminded African Americans that they had been pushed into an inferior position in society. For example, an African American had to step off the sidewalk at a white person's approach. These unwritten rules of conduct could be punished as severely as broken laws. For example, in 1948, the KKK killed an African American farmer because the farmer "drove too large a car."[10]

WHITE RIOTS AND THE NAACP

In 1908, a white mob in Springfield, Illinois, demanded the opportunity to lynch two jailed African Americans. One was accused of killing a white man, and the other was charged with raping a white woman. The woman later withdrew her claim. Discovering that the men had been moved for their protection, several thousand whites swept through the African American community, destroying businesses and homes, lynching two elderly black men, and injuring many more.

African Americans had created organizations before to protect their rights, but the Springfield riot gave them new urgency. A few months later, in February 1909, African Americans and whites formed the National Association for the Advancement of Colored People (NAACP). They tackled many injustices, including President Woodrow

The NAACP had its national office in New York City.

Wilson's approval of segregating African American federal employees during work.

However, white violence against people of color continued. In 1917, in Saint Louis, Missouri, a mob killed dozens of African Americans. Thousands of homes were burned down. Soon after, the NAACP organized almost 10,000 African Americans for a New York City protest. "Their tactic was silence," the organization's website states, "but their message resounded: anti-black violence is unjust and un-American."[11]

The problem of mob violence and lynching would not be soon solved. But the NAACP became a respected civil rights organization with many key accomplishments. One accomplishment was opening up military opportunities for African Americans during World War I. Six hundred

African Americans became officers and 700,000 registered for the draft.[12] But this success would lead whites to push back with a bloodbath known as the Red Summer of 1919, which extended from April to October.

Having served their country, African American soldiers returned home from war with pride and confidence. They believed they would receive better treatment but found hate and discrimination throughout the country. Many whites did not like seeing proud African American men in uniform and attacked them. Before the summer's end, large-scale attacks against African Americans swept through large cities, including Washington, DC. Federal troops, sent to restore peace in Arkansas, instead helped the mobs hunt and kill hundreds of African Americans, including women and children. Journalist Cameron McWhirter says the true number of victims of Red Summer isn't available, but that "hundreds . . . most of them black—were killed and thousands more were injured. Tens of thousands were forced to flee their homes." It was, he concludes, "the worst spate of race riots and lynchings in American history."[13]

THE CIVIL RIGHTS ERA

Two very different events propelled the country into the civil rights era of the 1950s and 1960s. The first involved 14-year-old Emmett Till of Chicago, who was visiting family in Money, Mississippi, in 1955. A 21-year-old white woman claimed Emmett made suggestive comments and grabbed her. Years later, at age 82, the woman confessed that she had lied. But the confession came too late. The woman's husband and brother-in-law took Emmett at gunpoint one night and tortured and killed him. When his body was found, he was unrecognizable.

His mother chose an open casket funeral so people could see what had been done to her son. The case "staggered the nation," reported the *New York Times*.[14] Yet an all-white, male jury declared the killers innocent. Afterward, the killers confessed to the crime in an interview, but legally they couldn't be retried.

The second incident occurred the same year, in Montgomery, Alabama. Seamstress Rosa Parks, who was the secretary of the Montgomery NAACP, refused to give her bus seat to a white rider and was arrested. At the time, young Dr. Martin Luther King Jr. was known only as the fiery new preacher at the city's Dexter Avenue Baptist Church. African American leaders chose him to lead a boycott of city buses. The whole community pledged to walk, bike, or carpool throughout the 13-month boycott. The boycott and its leaders caught the attention of the nation. King's home was bombed, though nobody was injured. Leaders were jailed, but the boycott continued.

Emmett Till's mother at her son's burial

Finally, a federal court determined that bus segregation was unconstitutional. One participant credited the success to "the nameless cooks and maids who walked endless

A Church Is Bombed

September 15, 1963, probably seemed like an ordinary Sunday to 11-year-old Denise McNair and 14-year-olds Addie Mae Collins, Carole Robertson, and Cynthia Wesley. The church service would soon begin at Sixteenth Street Baptist Church in Birmingham. They were inside when a bomb blasted through the building, killing all four girls and injuring many more, including Addie Mae's sister. The incident made it clear that even African American children were in danger and that churches weren't safe. Three KKK members were sent to prison for the crime, but it took years. The first one went in 1977, but the others weren't sentenced until 2001 and 2002.

miles for a year to bring about the breach in the walls of segregation."[15] It raised the hope and confidence of civil rights workers across the country. Many types of protests followed, including lunch counter sit-ins. The Student Nonviolent Coordinating Committee (SNCC) was involved in the Freedom Rides of 1961, which tested bus segregation throughout the South. At first, the SNCC supported nonviolent protests.

In Birmingham, Alabama, a series of peaceful sit-ins, marches, and boycotts occurred in 1963. Police used fire hoses and police dogs against men, women, and children, arresting many. President John F. Kennedy condemned the violent attacks. Later that year, hundreds of thousands of people gathered in the nation's capital for the March on Washington for Jobs and Freedom. There, King gave his now famous "I Have A Dream" speech. He expressed his hope for a time when his children would be judged by who they are as people rather than the color of their skin.

The protests, bloodshed, and sacrifice led President Lyndon B. Johnson to sign the 1964 Civil Rights Act. The act outlawed discrimination based on race, color, gender, religion, and national origin in public places, jobs, and schools. Similar laws had been passed, but this act promised federal enforcement. Of course, a law didn't automatically correct offenses or change hearts. Violence and discrimination continued, although positive changes happened gradually.

CONFEDERATE STATUES AND JIM CROW

In the 2010s, citizens protested against Confederate and other segregationist statues that stood on college campuses and in public places. Many have been removed. Yale University history professor David Blight notes that statues highlight events in US history that are important to people. He argues that people should put up additional statues that tell the other sides of the story to promote understanding. Others suggest that statues might be relocated to museums devoted to Confederate history. Statue supporters say that removing statues is an attempt to erase history. But most of these statues and monuments were placed during the Jim Crow era. Their message, says James Grossman of the American Historical Association, was that white supremacy still reigns.

The Rise of Black Power

Meanwhile, the Black Power movement began. Many people, growing tired of broken promises, were finished with accepting attacks without fighting back, as King advocated. Perhaps integration shouldn't be the goal, they thought. They turned their attention to defending and strengthening their own communities. Black Power, said author-activists Stokely Carmichael and Charles V. Hamilton, meant that people should feel pride in the color of their skin and help their communities. The Black Panther Party was formed in 1966. Some members of this organization had once belonged to the SNCC. Members of the Black Panther Party provided many services to African Americans in major cities, such as health screenings and breakfast and education programs.

Women in the civil rights movement had to fight the same sexist attitudes from within the movement as they found in society generally. However, many women persisted to become leaders in the movement. For example, in the Panthers, high school activist Tarika Lewis rose to various leadership roles. When five female leaders were later arrested along with three male Panthers, national leader Eldridge Cleaver condemned sexist attitudes within the Panthers, saying, "our women are suffering [as] strongly and enthusiastically as we are."[16]

The Panthers made it clear that they would no longer tolerate whites—civilians or police—terrorizing their communities; they were armed and ready to defend themselves. Such announcements, their black berets, and their militancy frightened many whites, who feared they meant to take over—though that was not the group's aim. However, their stand alongside King's talk of Christian love and justice seemed to offer the white power structure two choices: King's peaceful road or the Panthers' potentially violent road.

When King was assassinated in 1968, many people lost hope of peacefully resolving the United States' racial problems. Although laws had been passed and the number of sympathetic and informed whites was increasing, change was too slow, and abuses of African Americans continued. The problems created by slavery remained.

DISCUSSION STARTERS

- Why do you think many whites were so determined to prevent African Americans from having full citizenship?

- How do you think the many African Americans who fought for equality kept their courage in the face of violence and oppression?

- Have you heard about violent acts toward specific races that happen today? Explain them and why you think they happen in modern America.

CHAPTER THREE

ISSUES IN ENTERTAINMENT

The transatlantic slave trade carried millions of captive Africans to the Americas from the 1500s to the 1800s. During the journey, men running the slave ships would sometimes bring the Africans on deck to get air and sing and dance for exercise. Often hungry, sick, and despairing, the Africans weren't interested in dancing, but slavers whipped them if they disobeyed orders. For the slavers, watching captive people dance and sing—while sometimes playing instruments stolen from Africa—was entertainment. In addition, slaveholders often required enslaved people to dance and sing for guests. This practice of having black people serve as entertainers rather than in intellectual or other highly-skilled positions has continued for centuries.

Slavers would sometimes force their captives to entertain them.

It also pushed harmful stereotypes onto black people throughout in the United States.

STEREOTYPES IN ENTERTAINMENT

Starting in the 1830s, white entertainers drew on black stereotypes to create caricatures. They blackened their faces, made up their lips to look larger, and wore ragged clothing. This makeup application was called blackface. The most popular caricature was Jim Crow. By the end of the Civil War, minstrel acts headed to the Midwest. Because whites there seldom saw African Americans, the stereotypes became whites' beliefs.

In the 1840s, African Americans realized they could also work as minstrel entertainers. At first, the African American groups modeled themselves after the white imitations of black people to meet audience expectations. Gradually, African American performance troupes let go of black makeup and exaggerated features. By the mid-1800s, the African American Charles Hicks's Original Georgia Minstrels rose above other troupes both white and black. Hicks found talented people to join the troupe and the group went on tour. The minstrel shows declined around 1870, but waves of nostalgia for the days of unquestioned white supremacy would bring them back with white singers and actors in blackface throughout the 1900s.

Klansmen were depicted as heroes in *Birth of a Nation*.

Harmful stereotypes also made their way into film.
One prominent example of this can be seen in *Birth of a
Nation*, which came out in 1915. In the 2000s, *New Yorker*
writer Richard Brody said that the film's creator used
his remarkable talent in filmmaking to push destructive
stereotypes. Set in the South during the Civil War and
Reconstruction, it portrayed African Americans as not
worthy of citizenship. As the first full-length movie ever
produced, it drew large white audiences. It was also the
first movie shown in the White House. President Wilson

urged other leaders to see it, commenting, "my only regret is that it is all so terribly true."[1] The movie not only spread harmful stereotypes but led to violence as well. Lynchings rose dramatically.

Created with persuasive artistry, movies and television subtly shape viewers' opinions about people. Today, some movies and television shows feature African American men as frightening criminals, irresponsible fathers, and hard-bitten super cops. African American women are stereotyped as angry or sassy. Leading roles, when they are available to black people, are more likely assigned to light-skinned African Americans. In its 2018 *Hollywood Diversity Report,* the University of California at Los Angeles indicated that, despite gains, people of color were still underrepresented throughout television and film.

When that is corrected, stereotypical characters and storylines will likely decrease.

It is possible to follow the thread of misrepresentation and limited acting opportunities back to slave days. In her book *Ring Shout, Wheel About,* Katrina Dyonne Thompson notes that blackface "minstrelsy has often been viewed as the foundation of American entertainment culture."[2]

Cultural Appropriation

In the late 1800s, African Americans developed a musical style known as the blues. As pianos became cheap, African American Scott Joplin popularized the livelier ragtime, which lent itself to the foxtrot dance craze. Jass, or jazz, grew from these influences in the early 1900s. Each style was popular with African Americans, but that audience had limited funds. Whites owned most record companies and wanted to attract wealthier white customers. So the first jazz record was made by the all-white Original Dixieland Jass Band. Stephanie Hall, a specialist at the government organization American Folklife Center, said that these white musicians didn't want to admit where the musical style originated. "Far from crediting the New Orleans African American musicians they learned from, these young musicians claimed to have 'invented' jazz."[3] The Original Dixie Land Jass Band committed what is now called cultural appropriation, where members of one culture take another culture's creation and present it as their own.

Contemporary artists such as Miley Cyrus and Katy Perry have been criticized for adopting African American music, dance, speech, fashion, and more without crediting the source. Cyrus worked with various hip-hop artists, helping her to rise to stardom, only to criticize the whole genre later. *Huffington Post* writer Zeba Blay calls Perry "pop music's queen of appropriation." Blay points to "several live performances in which Perry has awkwardly attempted to recreate black dance moves and style."[4]

RACE, SPORTS, AND OWNERSHIP

Sometimes, plantation owners would gather to see two slaves wrestle or box. The slaveholder whose slave won the battle also gained ownership of the losing slave.

LENA HORNE: JAZZ AND JUSTICE

Jazz singer and actor Lena Horne was in demand for entertaining World War II (1939–1945) troops—but she wouldn't perform for segregated audiences. And when she saw African American soldiers seated behind German prisoners of war, she refused to perform and contacted the NAACP. As the first African American given a long-term Hollywood contract and the highest paid black actor in the 1940s, Horne refused roles disrespecting African Americans. She never missed making a stand for civil rights and respectful treatment, even when it hurt her career.

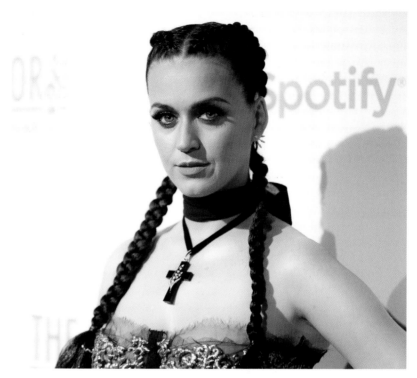

Katy Perry has been accused of styling her hair in an African American fashion.

As time went on, white people got angry when African American athletes beat white athletes. When boxer Jack Johnson, the son of slaves, beat the Canadian champion in a 1908 boxing match, writer Jack London pleaded for white athletes to win the title back for the white race. Two years later, when the white boxing heavyweight champion James Jeffries and Johnson faced off, Johnson won. In response, whites rioted throughout the country, killing dozens of African Americans.

In modern America, it seems that African Americans can dominate several sports without apparent backlash. However, reporter Tracey M. Lewis-Giggetts reminds people that racism still exists in sports. For instance, in basketball, Lewis-Giggetts points to incidents of changing grades and padding academic schedules to keep college athletes eligible to play, undermining their education. Some colleges don't seem to mind limiting African American players' futures. And an "ownership mentality," Lewis-Giggetts continues, leads to white outrage when

ATHLETES PROTEST

Athletes have used their spotlight to educate people on issues affecting the African American community. For example, the 1968 US Olympic gold and bronze medalist runners arrived at the awards ceremony shoeless, representing African American poverty. They each raised a black-gloved fist for strength and unity. Each also wore something around his neck to remember people who had been lynched. The protest cost them their medals.

Athletes since have used their position in the spotlight to protest social problems. San Francisco 49ers quarterback Colin Kaepernick began protesting in 2016. He sat through the national anthem. Kaepernick soon switched to kneeling. Other athletes joined him. President Donald Trump called the protests unpatriotic. But protesting the anthem was never Kaepernick's point. He was protesting frequent police shootings of often unarmed African Americans. Kaepernick opted out of his football contract with the 49ers and no other team picked him up.

a basketball star like LeBron James choses to leave his hometown team for greater opportunity.[5]

In addition, there are double standards when it comes to white and black athletes. For example, a 2013 study of basketball players noted that crimes committed by white players are viewed as "one-time lapses in judgment," while the same acts by black athletes "represent African American culture."[6]

There is also a racial gap in sports management. Mark Johnson, son of a former National Basketball Association player, notes, "the underlying systemic issues haven't changed all that much . . . very few of us are owning those teams. The good ol' boy network is still very much in effect."[7] Achieving racial equality in sports management could go a long way in establishing equality for players.

DISCUSSION STARTERS

- What effect do you think *Birth of a Nation* might have had on government leaders?

- How do false perceptions of people hurt them and the people who believe these perceptions?

- What instances of stereotypes do you see in the media today?

CHAPTER FOUR

EDUCATION: SEPARATE AND UNEQUAL

E ducation was dangerous for an enslaved person. Being caught with a book could lead to a whipping, having part of a finger cut off, or even death. Many places made educating enslaved people illegal. White people recognized that educated slaves could threaten their control over the slaves.

Thousands of enslaved people learned to read and write. They learned on their own or from each other. Some learned through white children they served. White ministers sometimes taught them to read the Bible. And sometimes slaveholders taught them or even hired teachers. Some people felt that

During segregation, African American students did not have the same access to resources as white students.

slaves should have some education, and that an educated person was more useful.

In the North, education for African Americans was disorganized before the Civil War. Pennsylvania had the Institute for Colored Youth for African Americans, which was established in 1837. The Ashmun Institute (later renamed Lincoln University) and Ohio's Wilberforce University offered just elementary and secondary education at first. Some whites in the North feared educated black people. Whites in Connecticut tried to burn down a school for African American girls in 1834. In addition, many whites would not send their children to schools with African Americans, nor would white colleges admit black students.

EDUCATION AND FREEDOM

After the Civil War, African American colleges appeared in the South, beginning with North Carolina's Shaw

THE ELIJAH MARRS STORY

Born into slavery in 1840, Kentuckian Elijah Marrs learned how to read. In 1864, he joined the Union army, taking 27 others along with him to earn their freedom. After the war, Marrs says, he became "a perfect curiosity to the white people . . . because I was the first colored school-teacher they had ever seen." His skills were in demand, and he moved more than 20 times for teaching jobs.[1] Because of Klan threats, he slept with weapons handy. Later, he cofounded Kentucky's first African American college, the Normal and Theological School.

University in 1865. During Reconstruction, thousands of African American schools dotted the South. Some of them were started by the Freedman's Bureau—a federal agency that helped black people after slavery ended. Others were established by missionaries. Many were started by African Americans who raised funds and built the schools themselves. More than 50 children often crowded into a classroom that might lack a blackboard and chalk.[2] Adults sat with the children, eager to drink in the education so long denied them.

Of the changes African Americans and white Republicans worked toward following the Civil War, free public education was among the most significant. Although white children were helped more by tax-supported schools, the thought that their tax dollars went equally to support African American schools fed white Southerners' anger over the changes they were experiencing. They didn't consider that generations of free work by enslaved people of all ages had built their wealth, or that African Americans' lack of opportunity to accumulate wealth entitled them to a good share of the funds. Whites were also wary of African Americans surpassing them in education and pushing for leadership positions.

Some states found ways to funnel most of the educational funds to white schools. As a result, African

Americans had to get along with worn, outdated texts and equipment cast off from white schools. They also attended run-down schools with poorly paid, often insufficiently educated teachers. The situation continued well into the 1960s.

Some African American schools helped keep Southern life largely unchanged from slave days. For example, Virginia's Hampton Institute, founded in 1868, taught African American teachers to prepare students for low-skilled jobs in which they would remain in service mainly to whites. A liberal education emphasizing critical thinking was, many whites erroneously thought, beyond black people's reach.

Jim Crow Education

As Jim Crow ruled the South, the vision of African American education serving as a pathway to equality faded. By 1900, just 36 percent of African American children from ages five to 14 attended school, and usually for less than six months each year.[3] Their academic schedule yielded to the cotton-picking season. Most students lived in rural areas and traveled to city schools. African American public high schools focused on industrial training. Like their Southern counterparts, many Northern schools remained segregated.

People worked to desegregate schools during the civil rights movement.

Despite the challenges, African American college enrollment soared in the 1920s. Participating in World War I had given returned black soldiers a new sense of possibilities and ideas of what might be gained through education. Many African Americans protested education aimed toward second-class citizenship. This forced a number of historically black colleges and universities to shift to liberal education. However, when the Great Depression gripped the country from 1929 to 1939, African Americans and poor white Southerners were hit the hardest. Already underfunded and poorly equipped, many African American schools shut down.

INTEGRATING THE SCHOOLS

In 1954, the Supreme Court determined that race-based school segregation was unconstitutional in the landmark case *Brown v. Board of Education*. The court ordered desegregation of all schools.

People working to integrate schools faced fierce opposition at every level. The governor of Arkansas sent the National Guard to keep African American students out of Little Rock Central High School in 1957. Six-year-old Ruby Bridges was the youngest to help integrate schools. In 1960, Federal marshals escorted her past angry mobs to and from the New Orleans school she attended. She was taught in a room without other children. Many schools shut down rather than integrate, and the federal government had to force them to reopen. Whites also fled to often hastily established private schools.

School segregation continued into the 2010s. As recently as 2018, white sections of Birmingham broke away to create separate, white school districts. Also, inner-city schools have high nonwhite populations based on housing patterns. The Education Trust, an organization promoting equal education for students of color and low-income students, released a 2018 report noting that schools in high poverty areas receive up to $2,000 less per student, despite the fact that those students tend to need more special programming.[4] As reporter Alvin Chang noted in 2018, "Racial segregation in schools was caused by white America's policies that kept schools and neighborhoods white-only. For black families, this meant their country engineered a second-class experience for them—one that put them in poor, segregated ghettos and poor, segregated schools."[5]

In addition to having a bleak environment, poor schools tend to lack equipment available in other schools, have less qualified teachers and weaker parent-teacher networks, and be less likely to offer advanced courses, according to Stanford University education professor Sean Reardon. Some people view education as just one of many systems reminding African Americans of their second-class citizenship.

RACISM PERSISTS

A National Bureau of Economic Research 2011 study looked at the outcome of desegregation on children born from 1945 to 1968. It showed that African American graduation rates increased for each year they spent in desegregated schools. Desegregating increases students' income and helps their health. It also gives all children an opportunity to experience a community that more closely mirrors the world they will enter.

Forced integration achieved the goal of getting African American students into better-equipped schools. But when those students face discrimination—whether conscious or unconscious—the benefit can be undone. For example, in 2016, Zion Agostini, a 15-year-old black student in New York, was often stopped by police and school officials before classes even started. In addition, students at his

TREATING WHITE AND BLACK STUDENTS DIFFERENTLY

Like most four-year-olds, Tyrone was rowdy, impulsive, and emotional. He was also curious and a booklover. But when Tyrone lost a game, he threw a ball at his playmate. Scolded by his teacher, Tyrone moved away, so she grabbed his arm. Tyrone pushed at her and was sent to the principal. The administration deemed him dangerous and suspended him. His story is not uncommon in the 2000s. When white students misbehave in such ways, notes scholar Kevin O'Neal Cokley, they aren't suspended. African American students made up only 18 percent of the preschool population in 2011–2012, a 2014 US Department of Education report found. Yet they made up 48 percent of those suspended from school, while whites made up just over 25 percent of the suspensions.[6] These trends were echoed in a 2016 report. The trends also continue into the higher grades.

school are required to go through metal detectors that can make them late to class. "The fact is now I'm [tardy] because I'm being scanned four times. . . . I missed whatever [the teacher] was explaining . . . and because of that I'm behind," Zion said.[7]

A 2016 study published in the *American Psychologist* shows that the stress racial discrimination causes could partly contribute to the achievement gap between black and white students. Writer Melinda D. Anderson summarizes the effects of discrimination on students by saying, "What emerges is a picture of black and Latino students whose concentration, motivation, and ultimately, learning is impaired by unintended and overt racism."[8]

DISCUSSION STARTERS

- What do you suppose the hopes of newly freed African Americans might have been in attending school?

- How do you think students are affected when their school lacks quality equipment and facilities?

- Why do you think so many whites didn't want integrated schools? Explain your answer.

DIVERSITY AND CHILDREN'S BOOKS

As schools integrated, librarian Nancy Larrick assumed publishers would create more diversity in children's literature. She studied 5,000 children's books published between 1962 and 1965, looking for progress. The title of her 1965 report reflects the problem: "The All-White World of Children's Books." In it, she accused publishers of "blatant racial bias" and serving "gentle doses of racism" to African American readers.[9] Most books neither mentioned nor pictured African American characters, so books reflecting their current lives were rare. Those that did often showed them with exaggerated features, with jet black skin, and in comedic and servant roles.

Although the number of books with African Americans dramatically increased in the 1960s during the civil rights movement, it soon dropped just as dramatically. African American author Walter Dean Myers stated in 1986 that, "for every 100 books published this year there will be one published on the black experience."[10] Children feel like outcasts when they don't see people like themselves represented, Myers comments. In 2017, the Cooperative Children's Book Center—a research library at the University of Wisconsin–Madison—reported that only 9.2 percent of children's books published were about African Americans, while 74.6 percent were about whites.[11]

Children's Books and People of Color[12]

In 2017, most children's books did not feature people of color.

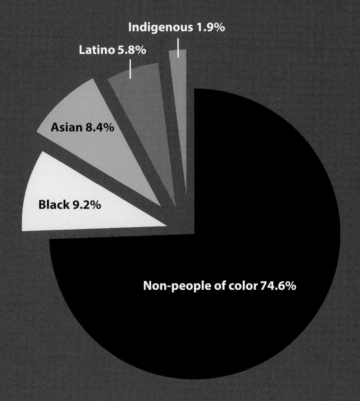

Indigenous 1.9%

Latino 5.8%

Asian 8.4%

Black 9.2%

Non-people of color 74.6%

Numbers do not equal 100% because of rounding

CHAPTER FIVE

HELP WANTED?

S lavery stirs images of field workers on Southern plantations. That was the most common situation, particularly in the 1800s. Enslaved field workers toiled for many hours under the hot sun with an overseer or slaveholder nearby, whip ready in case they slowed. In rice fields, they stood for long hours in water with mosquitoes buzzing about. Disease was a problem everywhere, but rice fields were the worst. No matter the crop, enslaved people were plagued by diseases and were poorly clothed and fed.

Some enslaved people worked in the plantation house. They worked as cooks, launderers, or personal assistants. These jobs meant they came into close contact with the slaveholder or his wife and were subject to his or her moods. Also, these slaves were always on call.

Enslaved people were forced to pick a daily quota of cotton for plantation owners.

Enslaved people also worked in cities in both the South and North. There, enslaved men might work in construction, in factories, or on the docks. They learned whatever skills were needed. Sometimes, they were allowed to hire themselves out. Although their income was the slaveholders', some were allowed to keep a portion of their earnings and, perhaps, one day buy their freedom.

SHARECROPPING

Once slavery was abolished, Union general William Sherman ordered that each former slave family receive 40 acres (16.2 ha) to support themselves. However, most never received this key piece to their freedom. Shortly after, President Andrew Johnson returned government-controlled land to its original owners. Instead of working for themselves, the newly freed people had to leave the land they had been given or work for the planters. The planters opposed change, so the working conditions offered little improvement over slavery.

Sharecropping began in the South as early as the 1870s. Under this system, men could rent land to work and pay the landowners in crops. This seemed positive, but because they had to pay for tools and other goods, it locked these formerly enslaved people into debt. Debt also accumulated through unexpected events, including illness, crop failure, lowered crop prices, and natural disasters. With few options, workers were forced to sign contracts, notes law professor Gloria J. Browne-Marshall, that "made it a crime for the laborer to refuse [to work] or escape" and reduced them to "involuntary servitude."[1] Once the contract was fulfilled, they might be forced to sign another or sentenced to hard labor in prison if they couldn't pay their debt. In Alabama, the wage for a sharecropping family was estimated at $0.65 daily even into the 1940s, making it impossible for the family to get ahead financially.[2]

SHARECROPPING FAMILY

Born in North Carolina in 1922, Willie Rufus Boyd grew up in a house that was "just a bunch of boards thrown together," he says.[3] Rats from the nearby dump invaded his family's house, devouring their food. From his bed, Willie could hear them chewing through the floorboards. One morning, one bit his toe. After many tries, they were finally able to get rid of the rats. Struggling to meet basic needs, families like Willie's found that highly treatable illnesses could mean disaster. The only African American doctor in the area served thousands of patients, so his horse-and-buggy visits were rare. Four of Willie's brothers died—one stillborn, two at birth, and the fourth at age four. It was a common story.

BOOKER T. WASHINGTON'S INFLUENCE

A famous Hampton Normal and Agricultural Institute graduate, Booker T. Washington was the son of an enslaved mother. Washington embraced the institute's message that African Americans should seek basic education and industrial skills. Unlike African Americans who pushed for leadership roles, Washington argued that equality would come once whites depended on blacks for skilled manual work.

Washington received applause at an 1895 Atlanta show, according to author Douglas A. Blackmon, when he stated that African Americans and whites could be separate socially yet work together for the country's progress. Washington encouraged African Americans to display their "mining, lumbering, and farming" skills.[4] These were "the very industries in which they remained most oppressed," Blackmon observes, through miserable working conditions, little to no pay, and, often, as forced laborers.[5]

Ibram X. Kendi is both a professor and the founder of the Antiracist Research and Policy Center at American University in Washington, DC. He suggests that Washington "was ingeniously playing the racial game," calming whites' fears of blacks fully integrating into society while also suggesting their usefulness to whites.[6] By appealing to powerful whites, he became an adviser to President Theodore Roosevelt and received funding for Tuskegee Institute in Alabama. The school offered basic education in English, history, and math. Men were trained to become farmers, carpenters, and brickmakers while women learned to be housekeepers and seamstresses.

Booker T. Washington thought that African Americans would be accepted into the white community over time.

The Tuskegee Airmen

The Tuskegee Airmen were famed African American World War II fighter and bomber pilots. Their accomplishments paved the way for thousands of military men and women. It was a time of segregated companies, barracks, and other facilities. The military even resisted recruiting African American nurses to care for white soldiers, despite a desperate need for medical personnel. The Airmen's officers were considered trainees, and the squadrons were commanded by whites.

For the air force, it was an experiment to discover if African Americans could be pilots and handle the demands of air battle. Airmen could also be technicians, navigators, radio operators, and more. Women were also employed in the Airmen, and they worked at jobs from gate guard and secretary to control tower operator and mechanic. Not only did the Airmen prove themselves, they were constantly requested to escort bombers because of their unmatched low loss record and awards for aerial combat.

Tuskegee had educated some 1,000 students by the early 1900s.[7] Alabama's white public colleges added together could not match its numbers.

Moving North and Joining Unions

Many black people moved north seeking better conditions beginning in 1914 as increasing industrial production, responding to the needs of World War I, promised jobs. Many did find unskilled laboring jobs—the same sorts of work they might have performed during slavery. But even Tuskegee graduates found they were unprepared for skilled work. And as they had been during slavery, African Americans were usually placed in the least desired and most dangerous jobs. Still, though often segregated while working, the conditions were generally an improvement over those in the South. By the 1940s, African American wages had risen significantly.

Skilled African Americans faced another problem: trade unions. These organizations fought for improved working conditions and pay and against competition from those nonunion members who would work for less money and fewer benefits. Since they were usually barred from joining unions, African Americans often weren't eligible to work in various industries. Some formed their own unions. In 1941, African American A. Phillip Randolph threatened to bring "50,000 Negroes to the White House lawn" unless President Franklin Roosevelt ordered an end to discrimination by unions, in hiring, and in the military.[8] The president relented, although he ignored the military, signing Executive Order 8802 to ban employment discrimination in federal jobs and also in companies that did work related to war. "For the first time," writes James Gilbert Cassedy for the National Archives, "the federal government admitted that blacks suffered from discrimination and that government had a responsibility to remedy it."[9]

STRUGGLING TO MAKE PROGRESS

During the civil rights era, President Lyndon B. Johnson established several laws meant to guarantee African Americans equal employment opportunities, particularly in the South. This led to more jobs and wage increases in 1965. Perhaps because of this, the number of African Americans moving north slowed.

But progress fell from 1979 to 1989. African American blue-collar workers' pay became much less than whites'. As new technologies developed, industries needed more production space, which they found in suburbs and beyond. Some African Americans were able to relocate with their industries. However, the new locations typically excluded black residents, and traveling to those jobs was difficult if not impossible for potential black workers.

City jobs increasingly required higher education, and in 1990, only 11.3 percent of African Americans had college degrees compared with 22 percent of whites.[10] However, during that same period, African American women's pay came closer to white women's as more black women received a higher education. In addition, African American women worked more frequently in full-time jobs than white women.

By the late 1990s, African Americans had narrowed the pay gap compared with whites. That's because the

In 2018, people continued to push for equal pay.

minimum wage increased and labor markets were pushed to not tolerate discrimination. Despite these things, the wage gap persisted. For example, in 2016 black men earned an average of 70 percent of white men's wages. Black women earned only 82 percent of what white women made.[11]

Jobs and Income Now

With increased openness and awareness of discrimination, many people think the United States has turned the

EEOC and African American Workers Today

The Equal Employment Opportunity Commission (EEOC) was started as part of the Civil Rights Act of 1964 to protect against discrimination in the workplace, voting, public accommodation, and schools based on race, sex, color, religion, and national origin. Today, it focuses on workplace issues and has broadened to include age, disability, and gender orientation discrimination.

In a 50th anniversary report, the EEOC noted that in 2014, it had remedied 30,429 cases of race-based discrimination. Those affected received $75 million, and changes were made in offending workplaces.[12] Some of these cases have gone to trial. For example, a Fort Myers, Florida, hospitality management company's CEO had the housekeeping supervisor fire the housekeepers, who were almost all African Americans, because he opposed working with them. When he realized the supervisor was African American, he fired her too, along with the only African American front desk worker. While not admitting guilt, the company agreed, among other things, to pay the fired employees $35,000 (divided between them) and conduct annual antidiscrimination training for management.[13]

corner. Slavery, they reason, was a long time ago, and a situation today's population never had to deal with. But slavery was built around the concept of work—certain types of work intended to serve whites' needs. Even as chains and whips fell away and African Americans attained greater education and strove to climb into positions of higher skill and authority, the attitudes of those holding the power to hire and fire did not correspondingly evolve. Political correspondent Jamelle Bouie cites 2017 research indicating that there was "no change in the level of hiring discrimination against African Americans over the past 25 years."[14] Furthermore, projections suggest that by 2020, the average "white household will own 86 times more wealth than its black counterpart."[15]

In January 2018, President Donald Trump tweeted he was happy to hear African American unemployment was at 6.8 percent—the lowest since the information was first collected in the early 1970s.[16] However, the Brookings Institution, a reputable research group, argues that the number doesn't include those who can't work or have given up searching. It is also still higher than whites' 3.7 percent unemployment rate.[17]

DISCUSSION STARTERS

- What troubles do you suppose an enslaved person assigned to work in the plantation house might encounter?

- Which do you think made better sense for newly freed African American men and women: training in trades or for positions of power? Which might you have pursued?

- Why do you suppose government officials have so often been reluctant to grant and enforce full rights and protections for people of color?

CHAPTER SIX

WHERE IS HOME?

I n 1736, an Englishman visiting Virginia and Maryland called enslaved people's housing "Huts or Hovels."[1] Their construction varied, the simplest being log cabins with dirt floors and two rooms at most. Field workers' cabins were often clustered in slave quarters near their work. Others slept at their workplace, such as in a stable, kitchen, or laundry.

The first housing for enslaved Africans was not homes but buildings for large groups of unrelated people. However, some slaveholders allowed families to live together in individual or two-family buildings. A 1797 visitor to George Washington's Mount Vernon saw the slave quarters and observed that "husband and wife sleep on a mean pallet, the

A higher percentage of African Americans live in poverty when compared with other racial groups in the United States.

children on the ground; [there was] a very bad fireplace, [and] some utensils for cooking."[2]

Many enslaved families were broken up as members were sold. Although marriage between enslaved people was illegal in Virginia until 1866, families formed. Thomas Jefferson considered that beneficial because families meant slave children who increased his wealth. During his life, Jefferson enslaved hundreds of individuals.

New Homes

After the Civil War, freed slaves were homeless if they left the plantations. The Southern Homestead Act of 1866 offered one remedy: allowing African Americans and whites to farm public land. However, whites quickly grabbed the best land. Rough hills and swamplands were left for African Americans. African Americans owning better

Slave Quarters, Freedmen's Home

Terry P. Brock is an archaeologist preserving former slave homes in Saint Mary's City, Maryland. Brock objects to calling the housing slave quarters. He says it excludes stories of residents after emancipation. One duplex he's working on, he says, "was a slave quarter for a quarter century, but a tenant home for 100 years."[3] Following slavery, residents who stayed on the plantations changed buildings to suit them. In the duplex's case, they cut down the dividing wall and added windows, wooden floors, and a bedroom. These changes suggest a family claiming ownership and making the home "a place of refuge," Brock said.[4]

land might be killed by whites who wanted it. Unable to read, many were also sold worthless deeds. Still, some African Americans did manage to acquire farmland.

Those who went north found themselves clustered in poor sections of town. Real estate contracts prevented whites from selling land or housing to people of color. Laws also prevented people of color from moving into white areas, except as servants living in white homes. When African Americans did manage to move into white neighborhoods, they often faced violence.

NEW DEAL, OLD DEAL

Often the government assisted in segregation and impoverished neighborhoods. Ghettos, or poor neighborhoods for minorities that are difficult to leave, formed generations ago and still exist today. Researcher Richard Rothstein argues that they formed not by residents' choice or by accident, but by a "racially purposeful policy that was pursued at all levels of government."[5] Much of this was coded into the laws and practices beginning in the 1930s.

Franklin Roosevelt was elected president in 1932, the third year of the Great Depression. He began the New Deal, a series of programs created to help Americans. Included in this deal was assistance with house payments and home loans. The assistance was much needed, but the New Deal didn't provide much help to African Americans, indicates Professor Ibram X. Kendi. Part of the problem was a rating practice known as *redlining*. Each neighborhood was color-coded, beginning with green for luxury homes. Red meant the neighborhoods were hazardous—or home to African Americans. If one African American family lived on a block, it was marked red. Hopeful home buyers who belonged to the growing black middle class couldn't get home loans based on the neighborhood's rating.

The government agencies administering the assistance programs gave single-family units priority in home loans over multiple-family units. However, the government agency providing loans for constructing suburban neighborhoods required that they exclude African American purchasers. City neighborhoods were not only largely ignored for home loans but also denied funds for repairs, so homes there became run-down. Even though rents were higher than in comparable white areas, services such as trash collection were more limited. Whites began to believe that slum conditions would arrive with African Americans if they came into white neighborhoods, strengthening white people's determination to block integration. When African Americans did move into formerly white areas, whites often left.

In 2019, the United States still had segregated neighborhoods, such as in Mechanicsville, Georgia.

Public housing, or tax-supported housing for low-income families, also began with the New Deal and has continued under various names. For generations, public housing cemented segregation. Although many of the neighborhoods selected for public housing had been integrated previously, authorities recreated those neighborhoods to be all of one race. Thus, concludes an NPR report, "public housing created racial segregation where none existed before."[6]

Segregated housing sends out ripples in all directions. Today, African American neighborhoods usually provide poor access to health care, transportation, and education. They also have higher crime rates.

UP IN SMOKE

By 1967, the cities were boiling over with frustration and rage over continuing discrimination, lack of jobs, and poor living conditions. Riots broke out across the country, often sparked by encounters with police. For example, in Newark, New Jersey, a peaceful protest followed the arrest and beating of an African American cab driver over a driving violation. A rumor spread that he had been killed. Though African American leaders called for calm, others began looting, rioting, and setting fires. It took five days to return the city to peace.

Why, some whites wondered, would African Americans cause such damage in their own communities? African Americans were frustrated. The presidentially appointed Kerner Commission revealed that racism was the root of the problem. "White institutions," it explained, "created [the ghetto], white institutions maintain it, and white society condones it."[7] The report suggested improving conditions in ghettos and encouraging broader integration in society, along with other changes affecting African Americans' lives. Otherwise, the report warned, "Our nation is . . . moving toward two societies, one black, one white, separate and unequal."[8] President Johnson

One destructive riot took place in Detroit, Michigan, in 1967.

had been hoping for a different answer and rejected his commission's findings, as did the majority of white people.

After two years of resistance, in 1968, Congress finally passed Johnson's Fair Housing Act to end racial discrimination in housing. However, winning Congress's approval of the act required compromise: 20 percent of the nation's housing, such as certain rental units, would be unaffected. Over time, many of the act's features meant to identify and penalize violations were whittled away.[9]

HOUSING TODAY

During slavery, African Americans were forced to live in clusters of ill-equipped shacks apart from the main house.

HOUSING FOR RENT OR SALE?

In 2012, more than 8,000 times in 28 cities across the country, a person of color and a white person asked realtors about housing. It was part of a study by the US Department of Housing and Urban Development and the Urban Institute. The testers claimed equal finances and jobs. Their report revealed that African American renters were given 11 percent fewer housing options and home buyers were shown 20 percent fewer homes.[10] All the testers reported courteous treatment, making the discrimination harder to detect.

While African Americans today generally live in better conditions, segregation is still evident in most cities and towns.

Dennis Parker, director of the American Civil Liberties Union Racial Justice Program, recognizes the positive changes since the Fair Housing Act, such as ending advertising that limits which races are welcome to apply for housing. Under President Barack Obama, cities had to provide evidence of fair practices to receive government funding. But people found loopholes. These included giving African Americans fewer housing choices and quoting higher rents and interest rates—even when their credit ratings were higher than whites'. Families with a single member having a criminal record are often denied housing.

The inability to buy quality homes has a lasting impact on African Americans' futures, states NPR's Terry Gross.

Most middle-income families' wealth is wrapped up in their homes. Through this large asset, they can get college loans, pay for care for aging parents and themselves, and leave money to their children. Deprived of this source of funds, many African Americans face nearly impossible obstacles in achieving those financial goals.

LIFE ON A TOXIC DUMP

"Where does one put a heap of toxic earth, laced with a chemical reputed to cause birth defects, skin and liver problems, and cancer?" asks writer Matt Reimann.[11] North Carolina chose Warren County because its occupants were "few, black, and poor," residents said during the late 1970s and 1980s.[12] Though residents protested, the landfill construction continued.

A 2017 report of the Environmental Protection Agency (EPA) showed the problem persists: pollution sources, it states, are more frequently located near communities of color. It may help explain the many illnesses that African American children suffer twice as often as white children.

DISCUSSION STARTERS

- Why is fair housing important to people of all races?

- What can people do to fight for fair housing?

- Which do you feel is more harmful, subtle racism or open racism? Explain your answer.

RACE AND WATER: FLINT, MICHIGAN

It was a common city scene: fire hydrants were opened and children played in the water on a hot summer day in 2014. But the water in Flint, Michigan, looked like coffee. It wasn't the first sign of trouble. Earlier, residents had noticed smelly, discolored water in their homes. Rashes and hair loss followed showering. Citizens complained to the city and were assured everything was fine, but it wasn't. In fact, water problems continued for more than two years. Among the problems were drawing water from the polluted Flint River; not replacing old, oversized pipes; and failing to follow the law in processing the water. The resulting medical problems included cancer, brain damage, and stunted growth, among other illnesses. In January 2016, Michigan's governor declared a state of emergency over the amount of lead in Flint's water.

A Civil Rights Commission report looked at the role race played in the problem. It reported, "The people of Flint have been subjected to unprecedented harm and hardship, much of it caused by structural and systemic discrimination and racism."[13] In other words, more care was taken in supplying clean water to nearby white-majority communities than in supplying this one. Had such a crisis occurred elsewhere, stated Karen Weaver, the mayor Flint residents elected in 2015, the response would have been quicker and more effective.

The National Guard passed out clean water to Flint residents.

CHAPTER SEVEN

POLICING, PROFILING, AND PRISON

During slavery, armed white men patrolled the countryside at night, searching for runaways or illegal religious or social gatherings. Through much of the South, a patroller could kill an enslaved person who resisted arrest, disobeyed orders, or threatened patrollers. The patrollers' story was the only side officials considered. Sometimes, having a pass or even being a freedman didn't help black people, and curfews overrode any permission a person might have. The patrollers could also enter slave quarters, searching for stolen goods, missing slaves, evidence of reading, weapons, or anything else

African Americans are more likely to be stopped and searched by police compared with white people.

From Slave Patrols to Police?

Many scholars believe that police departments evolved out of the slave patrols that controlled African Americans. Richmond, Virginia, for example—followed by other cities—launched its police department after an 1800 slave uprising. The patrollers, police support of the KKK, lynchings and other white supremacist activity, and discriminatory practices established African American distrust of police early on. Today, police shootings of African Americans, even when the victims were unarmed, nonviolent, and cooperating, often lead to no consequences for the police. These events confirm and further the distrust African Americans often have for the police.

that might suggest escape or revolt.

When emancipation came, the KKK took over the patrollers' jobs and quickly became a terrorist organization. Former Confederate officers, sheriffs, judges, and mayors joined in, making it clear that the law offered no shelter to African Americans.

Freedom Is a Crime

Freed from slavery, African Americans took to the roads by the thousands, searching for work and for family members sold away from them. The sight disturbed Southern whites, who responded with vagrancy laws, part of the Black Codes, which allowed officials to arrest people unable to prove they had homes or work. Then, if unable to pay their fines,

African Americans could receive long sentences of hard labor under slave-like conditions.

The loophole for this practice was written into the Thirteenth Amendment, passed in 1865: "neither slavery nor involuntary servitude, except as a punishment for crime . . . shall exist within the United States."[1] African Americans might also be arrested for things such as perceived misbehavior or insulting gestures. They were deprived of lawyers, the opportunity to testify, and the right to serve on a jury or face a jury of their peers. "For many Blacks," states law professor Gloria J. Browne-Marshall, "the criminal justice system was simply a mechanism for re-enslavement."[2]

LAW AND ORDER

Law professor Michelle Alexander observes that white Southerners interpreted the civil rights movement as "a breakdown of law and order."[3] That's because people were pushing back against segregation. During this time, civil rights protests, riots, and various crimes were lumped together as one problem. Even peaceful protesters were arrested, adding to the crime statistics, and so crime appeared to be rising.

Richard Nixon, who became president after Johnson, based much of his campaign on law and order. Some of Nixon's advisers said that Nixon believed people of color were at the root of society's problems and set out to appeal to racists in his campaign. Once in office, Nixon announced the War on Drugs in 1971. This was an effort to eliminate illegal drugs in the United States.

By 1990, the National Institute on Drug Abuse found roughly the same numbers of black and white drug users. However, more black people have been convicted of drug-related crimes than white people. The Drug Policy Alliance, a nonprofit organization that wants to change US drug policies, notes that this is because communities of color face discrimination in law enforcement. "Higher arrest and incarceration rates for these communities are not reflective of [more] drug use, but rather of law enforcement's focus on urban areas, lower income communities and communities of color," the organization says.[4]

The War on Drugs wasn't entirely responsible for the mass imprisonment of African Americans, though it was a large part of Nixon's crackdown on crime. President Ronald Reagan continued the policy throughout most of the 1980s. The mass imprisonment that began under Nixon caused the number of people in prison to nearly double to 627,000 under Reagan.[5] In the 2000s, lawmakers began considering alternatives to imprisonment

Nixon's War on Drugs continued to be a matter of debate in the early 2000s.

for nonviolent crimes, such as community service, treatment, and probation.

PROFILING AND POLICE BRUTALITY

With the larger percentage of African Americans arrested and imprisoned, police and other white citizens have come to imagine that being black fits the criminal profile. Thus, African Americans are more frequently watched, stopped, and questioned. Police are often called when someone perceives that a black person isn't acting as he or she should.

One instance of racial profiling in 2018 occurred at a Philadelphia Starbucks. Two black men were waiting for a friend when the store manager called police. The men

Rashon Nelson and Donte Robinson were victims of racial profiling when they were unfairly arrested at a Starbucks.

were arrested for trespassing. In this incident, charges were dropped, Starbucks apologized, and sensitivity training was given to Starbucks employees nationwide.

Too often, racial profiling ends in violence. In 2018, Stephon Clark, age 22, was shot eight times in his grandparents' backyard. Police mistook his cell phone for a gun. US police shoot and kill approximately three people daily, according to records kept by the *Washington Post* since 2015.[6] A 2018 *Atlantic* article notes that black men between the ages of 15 and 34 are nine to 16 times more likely to be killed by law enforcement than other groups.[7]

Videos taken of these shooting incidents have helped to publicize them and stir protests. As with Clark, police often say they felt their own lives were in danger. This claim seems to come up frequently when blacks are shot. Alexander believes that stereotypes of black men as aggressive and lawless can be connected

THE DEATH OF TRAYVON MARTIN

In 2012, 17-year-old Trayvon Martin was returning to his father's Florida home after visiting a convenience store. Seeing Martin, George Zimmerman, a neighborhood watch captain in the gated community, reported him to the police. Zimmerman ignored the police's instruction to stay in his vehicle and not approach Martin. Moments later, gunfire sounded. Zimmerman had a broken nose and scalp wound. Martin was dead. He had no weapon.

Rallies for justice for Martin swept the nation. Two months later, Zimmerman was charged with murder, but he was later declared not guilty. Martin's death and Zimmerman's trial helped to kick off the Black Lives Matter movement.

BLACK LIVES, BLUE LIVES, ALL LIVES?

The organization Black Lives Matter (BLM) was created in 2013. It called attention not only to killings of African Americans but also to empowering black community leadership and fighting injustice. Soon after the movement was born, two other cries arose: All Lives Matter and Blue Lives Matter. The first might seem reasonable—certainly all lives *do* matter. But, explains US politics lecturer David Smith, it "represents a refusal to acknowledge that the state does not value all lives in the same way."[8] White lives have always mattered; it is black lives that have been and are at risk—and often by police, or because police turn a blind eye. For this reason, the phrase Blue Lives Matter—a reference to police—is also a problem. Killing police officers has always been a serious crime. Smith adds that the Blue Lives Matter response is intended to create fear that BLM has called for a "war on cops," which is a false claim.[9] Both draw attention away from BLM's point.

back to the fears developed during and just after slavery. As a result, police and others are likely to overreact to African Americans' actions with violence, and African Americans are liable to receive harsher and longer punishments for real and imagined offenses.

ON THE STREET WITH A RECORD

People released from prison face many challenges. Employers are often unwilling to hire ex-convicts. Their education and employment history may be lacking, further limiting them. The majority, who were poor before prison, return to low-income areas with few jobs.

In addition, ex-convicts often lose a basic right of citizenship: the right to vote. A writer for PolitiFact reported in 2018 that millions of Americans can't vote because of felony convictions on their records. Since it's been shown that African Americans receive longer and harsher penalties for crimes than whites, many have been wrongly deprived of the right to make their voices heard through voting.

The decision whether to allow ex-convicts to vote is made by each state individually. Thus, a person may be allowed to vote in one state only to move into another and find his or her rights removed. In 2018, Florida decided to restore the voting rights of ex-convicts who have served time for most felonies.

DISCUSSION STARTERS

- What would be the result of feeling as though you can't turn to the police in an emergency?

- What types of racial profiling do you see used against other people of color, such as Hispanics?

- What might happen if people of color and whites work together for racial justice?

- Should those who have served their prison sentences have the right to vote? What differences might it make in the country?

CHAPTER EIGHT

WHERE WE ARE AND WHERE WE'RE GOING

S ome of the most historic buildings in the United States were built with slave labor— including the White House. Black people were not only forced to build the president's home but also forced to work there. Author Clarence Lusane wrote in his book *The Black History of the White House*, "For many African Americans, the 'white' of the White House has meant more than just the building's color; it has symbolized the hue and source of dehumanizing cruelty, domination, and exclusion that has defined the long narrative of whites' relations to people of color in the United States."[1]

Michelle Obama noted African American contributions to the United States in a 2016 speech.

First Lady Michelle Obama reminded people of the house's history in 2016. She was speaking about breaking barriers and her husband's historic presidential victory when she said to a large audience, "That is the story of this country . . . the story of generations of people who felt the lash of bondage . . . but who kept on striving and hoping and doing what needed to be done so that today I wake up every morning in a house that was built by slaves."[2]

Barack Obama's presidential election in 2008 marked a major step forward in African American leadership. It also brought hope to many people of color and whites who longed to see the United States deliver on its promise of liberty and justice for all. Many people said that the United States was becoming post racial—a society no longer troubled by racial discrimination.

However, a flurry of attacks against African

WORKING IN THE WHITE HOUSE

Lillian Rogers Parks spent many years of her life at the White House. As a young girl, her mother, who was a maid at the White House, took her to work. As an adult, Parks worked there as a maid and seamstress from 1929 to 1960. Parks wrote various books about her time in the White House, including *My Thirty Years Backstairs at the White House*, which provided insight into the presidential families but didn't highlight any major scandals. Parks's writings show an African American perspective of working in the president's home.

Americans followed the election, along with racist signs and vandalism. Some whites feared Obama's presidency would focus entirely on African Americans and claimed he hated whites. Author Dana Milbank wrote that Obama's election ignited "white insecurity."[3] This insecurity recalls slavery's end, when the first African American leaders were elected to local and national positions. White society had, for the most part, convinced itself that those of African descent were subhuman. While that belief has lessened somewhat over the generations, a sense of white superiority and, therefore, black inferiority made it hard for many whites to accept African American rulers.

Unconscious Racism

Racism continues to be an issue in the United States, and racism isn't confined to one race. Everyone has prejudices. Many prejudices are unconscious, and people may not realize their prejudices until they are confronted with them. Prejudices are absorbed along with other aspects of culture. But that whites created and supported a racist system to hold African Americans back is a historical fact. Whites' racial prejudices have a powerful system to back them, while blacks' prejudices are prejudices of individuals, without the force of culture and institutions behind them. It is important that people learn about racist systems and how they affect everyone, practice eliminating

The Cost of Slavery: Reparations

Many people have discussed the possibility of making reparations to descendants of enslaved people. Reparations are payments for damages. "When governments commit crimes against segments of their own population," says Randall Robinson, a civil rights activist and writer, "those governments have a continuing responsibility to address this and to provide restitution."[5] Funds, he feels, should go to education, training, and economic projects—not individuals.

However, African American economist Walter Williams opposes reparations, saying, "The American people have spent $6.1 trillion in the name of fighting poverty. We've had all kinds of programs trying to address the problems of discrimination."[6] Others feel that the debate alone is enough to inflame problems and would be better abandoned.

racism from their thoughts, and work toward a society that is safe and just and values all people.

Progress has been achieved over the country's long, troubled racial history. However, according to the Pew Research Center, 88 percent of African Americans believe more changes are needed for full equality. Nearly one-half doubt this will happen. Only 53 percent of whites, they found, believe more is required, but 89 percent of whites believe that it will happen.[4] Why the large gap in views? Most whites are not able to judge how prejudices rooted in the institution of slavery still impact African Americans. Not targeted by racism and not sensitized to notice slights, white people often don't see them, such as when a white person crosses the street rather than encounter a black person, or suddenly thinks to lock a car door when a black person is nearby. Listening to African Americans' experiences can help fill the gaps.

WHITE PRIVILEGE

Another, often unconscious, issue is white privilege. People of color, and African Americans especially, tend to experience treatment as second-class citizens in the United States—an inheritance of slavery. The reverse is true of whites. That is, they tend to experience first-class, or privileged treatment. Because of their skin color, whites can usually travel freely through society, expecting and receiving fair and respectful treatment. Their skin color will not create problems for them. It doesn't mean that they are never mistreated, simply that it is not as usual as it often is for African Americans. It also doesn't mean that whites don't struggle, that they didn't work for their success, or that they are wealthier than everyone else. Having white privilege doesn't mean someone is racist, either. It simply means that person has a built-in advantage in society.

Because they feel they are normal or average, most whites seldom think about how their race affects them. As writer Adia Harvey Wingfield describes it, "In most social interactions, whites [are] seen as individuals.

It is important for people with white privilege to acknowledge it.

Racial minorities, by contrast, become aware from a young age that people will often judge them as members of their group."[7] The actions of one, then, have an effect on others as whites assume an individual is typical of African Americans.

White privilege, writer Cory Collins explains in an article for *Teaching Tolerance Magazine*, is "the byproduct of systemic racism and bias."[8] It came from racism's long history and continues through current conscious and unconscious decisions. Individual whites can no more free themselves from white privilege than African Americans can free themselves from discrimination. However, as everyone becomes aware of how skin color gives them certain advantages or disadvantages, they are better able to recognize and fight racial injustice.

BRINGING THE HUMAN RACE TOGETHER

Slavery divided the US population into people and property, largely based on race. Even generations after the institution's demise, lingering prejudice continues to oppress black people. Professor Ibram X. Kendi argues that for racism to end in the United States, we must have "principled antiracists" in charge.[9] Other strategies, he feels, have not worked. Black people who have worked to improve themselves and their positions have experienced white backlash. Gains in civil rights came not so much from educating the public and stirring moral outrage, but from showing whites political and economic advantages. The best way to create change, he concludes, is to appeal to leaders' self-interest. Thus, people opposed to racism need to be in power.

Certainly, putting well-informed, just leaders in power who are committed to eliminating built-in systems of racism will help resolve this lasting injustice. But laws don't change the hearts that uphold racism. Relying on laws, important though they are, also makes average citizens think there is little they can do. In truth, there is much people can do toward creating a just society.

Constructive communication can help people understand others' experiences and points of view.

At the University of Wisconsin, Patricia Devine, director of the university's Prejudice Lab, and her coleader, Will Cox, advise people to build friendships outside their racial group and remember that individuals don't define the group. They should try to disprove stereotypes. "All of us are socialized into the system of racism," says Robin DiAngelo, a white educator exploring the meaning of whiteness in US culture. "Racism cannot be avoided."[10] Because of that, despite good intentions and awareness, people may sometimes say or do something insensitive or racist. It's hard for people to hear that they have offended others. Knowing that they were raised in a racist system should help them appreciate learning about mistakes as it makes them aware and promotes change.

Slavery and its aftermath have affected where Americans live, how they work and learn, and how they amuse themselves. Moreover, it has imposed on everyone a false sense of themselves by telling some that they are inferior and others that they are superior. Many people of all races want to rid society of racial injustices and heal from the institution that promoted human bondage.

DISCUSSION STARTERS

- How and why do you think prejudiced beliefs form?

- How likely do you think it is that the United States will overcome its racial problems? What will it take?

- What are some ways to break down barriers between different groups?

TIMELINE

1861

The Civil War begins to prevent the South from leaving the Union.

1863

On January 1, President Abraham Lincoln issues the Emancipation Proclamation, freeing enslaved people in states still rebelling against the Union.

1865

The Thirteenth Amendment is passed, ending slavery throughout the country; the Civil War ends.

1868

The Fourteenth Amendment is passed, granting former enslaved people US citizenship.

1871

The Ku Klux Klan Act allows the president to use military force against terrorist groups interfering with citizens' rights.

1896

In the court case *Plessy v. Ferguson*, the Supreme Court allows separate but equal services for white and black people.

1909

In February, the NAACP forms following mob violence against African Americans.

1954

The Supreme Court decides in *Brown v. Board of Education* that race-based school segregation is unconstitutional, leading to desegregation efforts.

1955

Fourteen-year-old Emmett Till is brutally murdered in Mississippi after being falsely accused of insulting and grabbing a young white woman; Rosa Parks refuses to give up her seat on a bus to a white person; the Montgomery bus boycott begins, led by Dr. Martin Luther King Jr.

1964

President Lyndon B. Johnson signs the Civil Rights Act, outlawing discrimination.

1968

Dr. Martin Luther King Jr. is assassinated.

1971

President Richard Nixon launches the War on Drugs, contributing to the mass imprisonment of African Americans.

2008

Barack Obama becomes the first African American elected president. He serves two terms.

SIGNIFICANT EVENTS

- After the Civil War ended, Southern states created Black Codes to essentially re-enslave black people and support white supremacy.

- Jim Crow laws promoted segregation of the races. Segregation of public facilities and schools typically meant that black people received unequal treatment compared with white people.

- The National Association for the Advancement of Colored People (NAACP) was formed in 1909. This organization exists today and tackles many racial injustices.

- The civil rights movement in the 1950s and 1960s fought against discrimination.

- In 2019, law enforcement continued to racially profile black people. This can often lead to violence and the killing of unarmed blacks.

KEY PLAYERS

- President Abraham Lincoln signed the Emancipation Proclamation, which freed some enslaved people.

- Booker T. Washington worked hard to provide education to black people.

- President Woodrow Wilson approved of segregating African American federal employees. He also helped popularize the racist film *Birth of a Nation*.

- Emmett Till's murder and Rosa Parks's activism ignited the civil rights movement of the 1950s and 1960s.

- Dr. Martin Luther King Jr. was a minister and civil rights leader.

- President Lyndon B. Johnson signed the 1964 Civil Rights Act as well as the Fair Housing Act of 1968.

IMPACT ON SOCIETY

In order to justify enslaving people, slaveholders convinced themselves and others that people of African descent were inferior and suited to slavery. Their beliefs soon translated into a system of laws, customs, and stereotypes that has lasted for hundreds of years and into current times.

QUOTE

"Our nation is . . . moving toward two societies, one black, one white, separate and unequal."

—*Kerner Commission Report, 1968*

GLOSSARY

abolitionist
Someone who works to put an end to slavery.

caricature
An imitation of someone by grotesquely exaggerating his or her characteristics.

curfew
A regulation that requires people to leave the streets at a certain time.

desegregation
The elimination of laws, customs, or practices under which people from different religions, ancestries, or ethnic groups are restricted to specific or separate public facilities, neighborhoods, schools, or organizations.

incarceration
To be imprisoned.

integrate
To make schools, parks, and other facilities available to people of all races on an equal basis.

lynch
To kill someone illegally as punishment for a perceived crime.

militia
A military force made up of nonprofessional fighters.

minstrel show
A staged event that offers dances and songs; often performed by white people in blackface.

plantation
A large farm or estate where crops such as cotton, sugar, and tobacco are grown, usually by laborers who live on the estate.

Reconstruction
The era after the Civil War when the Southern states rebuilt and reorganized.

segregate
To separate groups of people based on race, gender, ethnicity, or other factors.

stereotype
A widely held but oversimplified idea about a particular type of person or thing.

systemic
Part of an entire system.

white supremacy
The belief that white people are superior to all other races.

ADDITIONAL RESOURCES

SELECTED BIBLIOGRAPHY

Browne-Marshall, Gloria J. *Race, Law, and American Society: 1607 to Present.* Routledge, 2007.

Gates, Henry Louis, Jr., ed. *The Oxford Handbook of African American Citizenship, 1865–Present.* Oxford UP, 2012.

Rasmussen, Daniel. *American Uprising.* Harper, 2011.

FURTHER READINGS

Bakshi, Kelly. *Roots of Racism.* Abdo, 2018.

Harris, Duchess. *Fighting Stereotypes in Sports.* Abdo, 2019.

Harris, Duchess. *The US Prison System and Prison Life.* Abdo, 2020.

ONLINE RESOURCES

To learn more about the impact of slavery in America, please visit **abdobooklinks.com** or scan this QR code. These links are routinely monitored and updated to provide the most current information available.

MORE INFORMATION

For more information on this subject, contact or visit the following organizations:

NATIONAL ASSOCIATION FOR THE ADVANCEMENT OF COLORED PEOPLE (NAACP)

4805 Mt. Hope Dr.
Baltimore, MD 21215
877-622-2798
naacp.org

The NAACP is the country's oldest civil rights organization. It is devoted to promoting equality and ending prejudice.

SOUTHERN POVERTY LAW CENTER

400 Washington Ave.
Montgomery, AL 36104
888-414-7752
splcenter.org

The Southern Poverty Law Center promotes tolerance, understanding, and justice.

SOURCE NOTES

CHAPTER 1. FIGHTING TO BE FREE

1. Daniel Rasmussen. *American Uprising*. Harper, 2011. 49.

2. Henry Louis Gates Jr. "Why Was Cotton King?" *PBS*, n.d., pbs.org. Accessed 6 Feb. 2019.

3. Rasmussen, *American Uprising*, 2.

4. "Nat Turner's Rebellion." *PBS*, n.d., pbs.org. Accessed 6 Feb. 2019.

5. "Nat Turner's Rebellion."

6. Christopher Beagan. "Freedom's Fortress." *National Park Service*, n.d., nps.gov. Accessed 6 Feb. 2019.

CHAPTER 2. THE LONG ROAD TOWARD EQUALITY

1. Eric Foner. "South Carolina's Forgotten Black Political Revolution." *Slate*, 31 Jan. 2018, slate.com. Accessed 6 Feb. 2019.

2. Charles Lane. *The Day Freedom Died*. Henry Holt and Co., 2008. 3.

3. Lane, *The Day Freedom Died*, 3–4.

4. Lane, *The Day Freedom Died*, 3–4.

5. Elizabeth Kiefer. "How the Women of the KKK Helped Architect a Hate Movement." *Refinery29*, 18 Oct. 2017, refinery29.com. Accessed 6 Feb. 2019.

6. "Lynching in America." *Equal Justice Initiative*, n.d., lynchinginamerica.eji.org. Accessed 6 Feb. 2019.

7. "Lynching in America."

8. "Lynching in America: Confronting the Legacy of Racial Terror." *Equal Justice Initiative*, n.d., eji.org. Accessed 6 Feb. 2019.

9. Melvin I. Urofsky. "Jim Crow Law." *Encyclopedia Britannica*, n.d., britannica.com. Accessed 6 Feb. 2019.

10. Stetson Kennedy. *Jim Crow Guide to the U.S.A.* U of Alabama P, 1990. 207.

11. "Silent Protest Parade Centennial." *NAACP*, n.d., naacp.org. Accessed 6 Feb. 2019.

12. "NAACP Timeline." *Eastern Illinois University Chapter of the NAACP*, n.d., castle.eiu.edu. Accessed 6 Feb. 2019.

13. Eric Arnesen. "'Red Summer: The Summer of 1919 and the Awakening of Black America' by Cameron McWhirter." *Chicago Tribune*, 18 Nov. 2011, chicagotribune.com. Accessed 6 Feb. 2019.

14. Alan Blinder. "US Reopens Emmett Till Investigation, Almost 63 Years after His Murder." *New York Times*, 12 July 2018, nytimes.com. Accessed 6 Feb. 2019.

15. "Montgomery Bus Boycott." *Stanford University*, n.d., kinginstitute.stanford.edu. Accessed 6 Feb. 2019.

16. Ashely Farmer, et al. "Women in the Black Panther Party." *ISR*, n.d., isreview.org. Accessed 6 Feb. 2019.

CHAPTER 3. ISSUES IN ENTERTAINMENT

1. Richard Wormser. "D. W. Griffith's *The Birth of a Nation* (1915)." *Thirteen*, n.d., thirteen.org. Accessed 8 Feb. 2019.

2. Katrina Dyonne Thompson. *Ring Shout, Wheel About: The Racial Politics of Music and Dance in North American Slavery*. U of Illinois P, 2017. 190.

3. Stephanie Hall. "The Painful Birth of Blues and Jazz." *Library of Congress*, 24 Feb. 2017, loc.gov. Accessed 8 Feb. 2019.

4. Zeba Blay. "We Need to Talk about Katy Perry." *Huffington Post*, 24 May 2017, huffingtonpost.com. Accessed 8 Feb. 2019.

5. Tracey M. Lewis-Giggetts. "When Black Players Were Basketball Slaves: Has the NBA Really Changed?" *Ebony*, 8 June 2016, ebony.com. Accessed 8 Feb. 2019.

6. Kwame J. A. Agyemang and John N. Singer. "Race in the Present Day." *Journal of African American Studies*, vol. 18, no. 1, 2014. jstor.org. Accessed 8 Feb. 2019.

7. Lewis-Giggetts, "When Black Players Were Basketball Slaves."

CHAPTER 4. EDUCATION: SEPARATE AND UNEQUAL

1. Jonathan Garcia. "Elijah P. Marrs, b. 1840." *Documenting the American South*, n.d., docsouth.unc.edu. Accessed 8 Feb. 2019.

2. Eric Foner and Olivia Mahoney. "America's Reconstruction." *Digital History*, n.d., digitalhistory.uh.edu. Accessed 8 Feb. 2019.

3. Joy Ann Williamson-Lott, Linda Darling-Hammond, and Maria E. Hyler. *Education and the Quest for African American Citizenship*. Oxford U P, 2012. 598.

4. Lauren Camera. "In Most States, Poorest School Districts Get Less Funding." *US News & World Report*, 27 Feb. 2018, usnews.com. Accessed 8 Feb. 2019.

5. Alvin Chang. "The Data Proved That School Segregation Is Getting Worse." *Vox*, 5 Mar. 2018, vox.com. Accessed 8 Feb. 2019.

6. Esther Canty-Barnes. "Racial Inequality Starts Early—in Preschool." *Conversation*, 13 July 2016, theconversation.com. Accessed 8 Feb. 2019.

7. Melinda D. Anderson. "How the Stress of Racism Affects Learning." *Atlantic*, 11 Oct. 2016, theatlantic.com. Accessed 8 Feb. 2019.

8. "How the Stress of Racism Affects Learning."

9. Kenneth B. Kidd and Joseph T. Thomas Jr., eds. *Prizing Children's Literature: The Cultural Politics of Children's Book Awards*. Routledge, 2017. 88.

10. Kidd and Thomas, *Prizing Children's Literature*, 89.

11. Lisa Philip. "Her Kids Didn't See Themselves in Books. So This NC Mom Started Writing." *North Carolina Public Radio*, 17 July 2018, wunc.org. Accessed 8 Feb. 2019.

12. Philip, "Her Kids Didn't See Themselves in Books."

CHAPTER 5. HELP WANTED?

1. Gloria J. Browne-Marshall. *Race, Law, and American Society: 1607–Present*. Routledge, 2013. 58.

2. Kenneth E Phillips. "Sharecropping and Tenant Farming in Alabama." *Encyclopedia of Alabama*, 28 July 2008, encyclopediaofalabama.org. Accessed 8 Feb. 2019.

3. Robert Samuel Smith. *Race, Labor & Civil Rights*. Louisiana State U P, 2018. 35–37.

4. Douglas A. Blackmon. *Slavery by Another Name: The Re-Enslavement of Black Americans from the Civil War to World War II*. Anchor, 2009. 142.

5. Blackmon, *Slavery by Another Name*, 142.

6. Ibram X. Kendi *Stamped from the Beginning: The Definitive History of Racist Ideas in America*. Nation, 2016. 284.

7. Candice Norwood. "The Legacy of Booker T. Washington Revisited." *NPR*, 5 Mar. 2015, npr.org. Accessed 8 Feb. 2019.

8. "Executive Order 8802." *Our Documents*, n.d., ourdocuments.gov. Accessed 8 Feb. 2019.

9. James Gilbert Cassedy. "African Americans and the American Labor Movement." *National Archives*, n.d., archives.gov. Accessed 8 Feb. 2019.

10. Thomas N. Maloney. "African Americans in the Twentieth Century." *Economic History Association*, n.d., eh.net. Accessed 8 Feb. 2019.

11. Eshe Nelson. "The Growing Gap between Black and White Workers' Wages in the US Is Getting Harder to Explain." *Quartz*, 11 Sept. 2017, qz.com. Accessed 8 Feb. 2019.

12. "African-Americans in the American Workforce." *US Equal Employment Opportunity Commission*, n.d., eeoc.gov. Accessed 8 Feb. 2019.

13. "Hospman Settles EEOC Race Discrimination Lawsuit." *US Equal Employment Opportunity Commission*, 27 Jan. 2017, eeoc.gov. Accessed 8 Feb. 2019.

14. Jamelle Bouie. "The Wealth Gap between Whites and Blacks Is Widening." *Slate*, 17 Sept. 2017, slate.com. Accessed 8 Feb. 2019.

15. Bouie, "The Wealth Gap between Whites and Blacks Is Widening."

16. Brakkton Booker. "President Trump 'So Happy' Black Unemployment Rate at a Historic Low." *NPR*, 6 Jan. 2018, npr.org. Accessed 8 Feb. 2019.

17. Booker, "President Trump 'So Happy' Black Unemployment Rate at a Historic Low."

CHAPTER 6. WHERE IS HOME?

1. Dennis J. Pogue and Douglas Sanford. "Slave Housing in Virginia." *Encyclopedia Virginia*, n.d., encyclopediavirginia.org. Accessed 8 Feb. 2019.

2. "Slave Quarters." *George Washington's Mount Vernon*, n.d., mountvernon.org. Accessed 8 Feb. 2019.

3. "On Slave and Tenant Quarters and the Importance of Naming." *Terry P. Brock*, 23 June 2013, terrypbrock.com. Accessed 8 Feb. 2019.

4. "On Slave and Tenant Quarters and the Importance of Naming."

5. "Historian Says Don't 'Sanitize' How Our Government Created Ghettos." *NPR*, 14 May 2015, npr.org. Accessed 8 Feb. 2019.

6. "Historian Says Don't 'Sanitize' How Our Government Created Ghettos."

7. Alice George. "The 1968 Kerner Commission Got It Right, but Nobody Listened." *Smithsonian*, 1 Mar. 2018, smithsonianmag.com. Accessed 8 Feb. 2019.

8. *The Kerner Report*. Princeton U P, 2016. xxvii.

9. Douglas S. Massey. "The Legacy of the 1968 Fair Housing Act." *Sociological Forum*, vol. 30, no. 1, 2015, ncbi.nlm.nih.gov. Accessed 8 Feb. 2019.

10. Gene Demby. "For People of Color, a Housing Market Partially Hidden from View." *NPR*, 17 June 2013, npr.org. Accessed 8 Feb. 2019.

11. Matt Reimann. "The EPA Chose This County for a Toxic Dump Because Its Residents Were 'Few, Black, and Poor.'" *Timeline*, 2 Apr. 2017, timeline.com. Accessed 8 Feb. 2019.

12. Reimann, "The EPA Chose This County for a Toxic Dump Because Its Residents Were 'Few, Black, and Poor.'"

13. Steve Almasy and Laura Ly. "Flint Water Crisis: Report Says 'Systemic Racism' Played Role." *CNN*, 18 Feb. 2017, cnn.com. Accessed 8 Feb. 2019.

CHAPTER 7. POLICING, PROFILING, AND PRISON

1. "13th Amendment." *Cornell Law School*, n.d., law.cornell.edu. Accessed 8 Feb. 2019.

2. Gloria J. Browne-Marshall. *Race, Law, and American Society: 1607–Present*. Routledge, 2013. 57.

3. Michelle Alexander. *The New Jim Crow*. New Press, 2012. 40.

4. "Race and the Drug War." *Drug Policy Alliance*, n.d., drugpolicy.org. Accessed 8 Feb. 2019.

5. James Cullen. "The History of Mass Incarceration." *Brennan Center for Justice*, 20 July 2018, brennancenter.org. Accessed 8 Feb. 2019.

6. Wesley Lowery. "Police Are Still Killing Black People. Why Isn't It News Anymore?" *Washington Post*, 16 Mar. 2018, washingtonpost.com. Accessed 8 Feb. 2019.

7. Olga Khazan. "In One Year, 57,375 Years of Life Were Lost to Police Violence." *Atlantic*, 8 May 2018, theatlantic.com. Accessed 6 Mar. 2019.

8. David Smith. "The Backlash against Black Lives Matter Is Just More Evidence of Injustice." *Conversation*, 31 Oct. 2017, theconversation.com. Accessed 8 Feb. 2019.

9. Smith, "The Backlash against Black Lives Matter Is Just More Evidence of Injustice."

CHAPTER 8. WHERE WE ARE AND WHERE WE'RE GOING

1. "The 'Black History' of America's White House." *NPR*, 3 Feb. 2011, npr.org. Accessed 8 Feb. 2019.

2. Olivia B. Waxman. "Michelle Obama Reminded Us That Slaves Built the White House. Here's What to Know." *Time*, 26 July 2016, time.com. Accessed 8 Feb. 2019.

3. Dana Milbank. "Milbank: Was Obama Ahead of His Time, or Are We Behind Ours?" *Herald Net*, 4 June 2018, heraldnet.com. Accessed 8 Feb. 2019.

4. "On Views of Race and Inequality, Blacks and Whites Are Worlds Apart." *Pew Research Center*, 27 June 2016, pewsocialtrends.org. Accessed 8 Feb. 2019.

5. "20/20: Americans Debate Reparations for Slavery." *ABC News*, 23 Mar. 2018, abcnews.com. Accessed 20 Oct. 2018.

6. "20/20: Americans Debate Reparations for Slavery."

7. Adia Harvey Wingfield. "Color-Blindness Is Counterproductive." *Atlantic*, 13 Sept. 2015, theatlantic.com. Accessed 8 Feb. 2019.

8. Cory Collins. "What Is White Privilege, Really?" *Teaching Tolerance*, n.d., tolerance.org. Accessed 8 Feb. 2019.

9. Ibram X. Kendi *Stamped from the Beginning: The Definitive History of Racist Ideas in America*. Nation, 2016. 510.

10. Robin J. DiAngelo. *White Fragility: Why It's So Hard for White People to Talk about Racism*. Beacon, 2018. 142.

INDEX

DUCHESS HARRIS, JD, PHD

Dr. Harris is a professor of American Studies at Macalester College and curator of the Duchess Harris Collection of ABDO books. She is also the coauthor of the titles in the collection, which features popular selections such as *Hidden Human Computers: The Black Women of NASA* and series including News Literacy and Being Female in America.

Before working with ABDO, Dr. Harris authored several other books on the topics of race, culture, and American history. She served as an associate editor for *Litigation News*, the American Bar Association Section of Litigation's quarterly flagship publication, and was the first editor in chief of *Law Raza*, an interactive online journal covering race and the law, published at William Mitchell College of Law. She has earned a PhD in American Studies from the University of Minnesota and a JD from William Mitchell College of Law.

GAIL RADLEY

Gail Radley is the author of 28 books for young people and numerous articles for adults. She also teaches part time at Stetson University in DeLand, Florida. In the 1960s, she belonged to a civil rights group in the Washington, DC, area and is currently a member of the NAACP.